Escape From New Cheese City

How the Rats Control the Cheese
and Why the Middle Class Always Pays

By **Eric F. Gilbert**

VizzyBrand Publishing

ISBN: 978-1-968365-11-0

Escape From New Cheese City: How the Rats
Control the Cheese and Why the Middle Class
Always Pays

Published by VizzyBrand Publishing
United States of America

This is a work of allegory. Any resemblance to real
persons or real cities is coincidental.

DEDICATION

This book is dedicated to my mother, who—when
I was only five years old—taught me the greatest
life lesson of all:

**If you want something badly enough,
you will figure out a way
to make it happen.**

Why This Book Exists

We are living in a world where everyone is fighting over cheese.

People want free cheese.
 People resent the people who took more cheese.
 People blame the people who make the cheese.
 People elect Rats who promise to redistribute cheese.
 And the middle class—the Carriers—end up footing the bill for everybody's cheese.

The wealthy Keepers don't pay taxes like you do.
 The poor are encouraged to depend on programs.
 The Rats win by dividing everyone else.
 And the Carriers keep working harder for less.

We've built a society where dependency is rewarded, productivity is punished, and mediocrity is normalized—while the people who actually keep the country running are suffocating under the load.

We keep voting for promises that make problems worse.
 We keep asking the wrong questions.
 We keep believing someone else will fix it.

Nobody is coming.

I didn't write this to tell you what to think.
 I wrote it to help you see what you've been living through.

You won't change New Cheese City.
 But you *can* leave it.

You can build your own runway.
 You can become a Mover.
 You can create a life the Rats cannot control.

And it starts right now.

Why I Chose a Fable

Statistics divide people.
 Stories unite them.

Stories bypass defenses.
 They hit memory, emotion, and truth at the same time.

And the truth is this:

Most people aren't stuck because they're lazy.
 They're stuck because they were trained to depend on the maze.

When I was a kid, I begged my mother for a three-wheeler. She didn't say "no."
 She said, *"If you really want it, figure out a way to buy it."*

That line shaped my entire life.

But millions are never taught that.
 They're taught to wait.
 To depend.
 To vote for free cheese.

So I wrote this book as a modern fable—not to simplify reality, but to expose it.

New Cheese City is not fictional.
 It's everywhere.

In your paycheck.
 Your taxes.
 Your elections.
 Your frustrations.
 Your bills.
 Your neighborhood.
 Your daily grind.

Until you see the system from above, you cannot escape it.

That's what this story is for.

TABLE OF CONTENTS

"You don't escape the maze by
running faster.
You escape by learning who
controls the cheese."

THE MAZE DREAM

I was running through a maze.

Not a cute, wooden fairground maze.
 A concrete maze. Cold. Damp. Windowless.
 The walls were tall enough to block out the sky.

And everywhere—echoing through the narrow
corridors—
 I heard squeaking.
 Laughing.
 Whispers.
 Deals being made in the dark.

At every turn, signs pointed in different directions:

FREE CHEESE THIS WAY
RICH PEOPLE STEALING YOUR CHEESE
YOU DESERVE MORE CHEESE
YOUR NEIGHBOR HAS EXTRA CHEESE
THE RATS WILL PROTECT YOUR
CHEESE

I kept running.
Every path I chose led back to the same place:

A giant round table covered in cheese.

But I wasn't allowed near it.

At the table sat tall, well-fed Rats in suits—
counting cheese, dividing cheese, arguing about
cheese, promising cheese they didn't own, and
giving away cheese they didn't earn.

Behind them stood the Keepers: quiet, wealthy,
untouchable.
They didn't fight for cheese.
They *owned* the maze.

Then there were the Takers: pushing, begging,
demanding, rioting—doing anything to get their
free share of cheese.

The Carriers marched in circles carrying giant
wheels of cheese on their backs, sweating,
breaking, exhausted, just to get a small piece of
cheese at the end of the long hard day.

And then there were the Movers.
 Who… didn't even touch the maze walls.
 They found ladders.
 They climbed out.
 They walked above the system while everyone
else kept running inside it.

I turned a corner—
 slammed into a dead end—
 and suddenly a Rat in a bright red tie leaned over
me and whispered:

**"You don't escape the maze by running faster.
 You escape by learning who controls the
cheese."**

I jolted awake—

CHAPTER 1

Terminal C:
Where America Comes to Fight Itself

The dream was still clinging to my brain as I stood in line at Terminal C, waiting for my delayed flight.

The airport was packed—shoulder to shoulder, frustrated faces, overpriced snacks, crying kids, exhausted workers.

A perfect snapshot of America.

I squeezed into a narrow seat near the gate.
 As I sat, I noticed a little boy in the gift shop next to us pointing at a neck pillow shaped like a block of cheese.

He wanted it.
 Badly.

His mother said no.

So he threw himself on the floor, kicking, screaming, demanding—the whole meltdown package.

I leaned slightly toward the exhausted guy sitting next to me and said:

"That reminds me of the time I told my mom I wanted a three-wheeler when I was a kid."

He chuckled.
 "Let me guess—she didn't buy it?"

"Nope. She said, *If you really want it, figure out a way to buy it.*"

He nodded slowly. "Wish more parents said that."

We both watched as the child screamed louder.
 The mother apologized to the cashier.

People stared.
People judged.

The guy beside me sighed. "Kids these days…"

I shook my head.
"It's not the kid.
It's the system."

He turned to me.
"The system?"

I gestured around the terminal.

"You see all these people?
I'm pretty sure every type of person in the cheese economy is in this room right now."

He frowned. "Cheese economy?"

"Yep," I said. "Let me show you."

I pointed to the kid in the shop.
"He's a Taker-in-training. Already learning that screaming gets you cheese."

Then I nodded toward a woman with a laptop on her knees, exhausted, juggling emails and snacks for two kids.

"She's a Carrier. Works nonstop. Pays the taxes. Gets almost nothing in return."

Then I pointed toward the exclusive lounge up the escalator—visible through frosted glass.

"That's where the Keepers are. They're not waiting. They're not stressed. They're not in this line. They're not breaking their backs. And because of how their money is structured, most of them aren't paying the taxes she is."

The guy's eyebrows lifted. "Okay… and the Rats?"

I smirked and nodded again toward the hallway.

Right on cue, a local politician walked through—smiling, shaking hands, pretending to be "one of the people," all while wearing a suit more expensive than half the terminal's yearly income.

"There's your Rat," I said.
 "Always shows up where the crowds gather, begging for attention, promising cheese he didn't produce."

The guy laughed.
 "This is wild. What are you saying—that this airport is…?"

I turned toward him.

"This isn't a mess," I said softly.

"This is **New Cheese City**."

He stared at me.

"Welcome," I added, "to the place where everyone wants cheese…
 but nobody understands who really pays for it."

CHAPTER 2

What Is Cheese?

"Okay," the guy beside me said, "if this airport is New Cheese City… then what exactly is *cheese*?"

I smiled, because that's the right question.

"Cheese," I said, "is anything people want but don't know how to earn."

He waited.

"It's money," I continued.
"It's housing.
It's food.
It's healthcare.

It's opportunity.
It's safety.
It's stability.
It's a future.
It's the hope that tomorrow can be better than today."

Cheese is **whatever they believe someone else owes them.**

He nodded slowly. "So the kid screaming in the shop…"

"Wants cheese," I said. "And he's being trained young to get it by demanding."

I pointed toward a different woman now—one in scrubs, slumped in a chair after what was clearly a long shift.

"She wants cheese too. But she doesn't demand it. She *earns* it with her back, her time, her health, her sanity."

He followed my gaze. "And the people in the lounge?"

"They want cheese, but they don't earn it with sweat. They earn it with strategy."

He blinked. "Strategy?"

"Keepers don't fight for cheese. They *own* the cheese factory. They control the maze the rest of us run through."

He leaned back, thinking.

"So cheese isn't really cheese."

"No," I said. "It's what cheese represents: **the reward. The comfort. The payout. The win.**"

He smirked. "So what are we doing? Just watching different people chase it?"

I nodded.

"And I'm going to show you why some people stay stuck chasing crumbs while others walk through the airport without a care in the world."

He chuckled nervously. "Alright. I'm listening."

"Good," I said. "Because once you understand cheese…
 you understand this entire country."

CHAPTER 3

The Five Kinds of People in a Cheese Economy

"Alright," the guy said. "You said everyone in here fits into a group. Tell me the groups."

"Sure," I replied. "There are only five."

I pointed again to the little boy still recovering from his meltdown in the shop.

1. Takers

"Takers believe they're owed cheese simply because they want it.
They don't create.
They don't build.

They don't contribute.
They depend."

He nodded. "We all know people like that."

"And New Cheese City trains them to stay that way," I said. "Generations deep."

I pointed to the exhausted workers, the people juggling two phones, the ones on lunch breaks answering emails.

The Carrier leaned back. "You know, you keep calling them Takers, but not all of them sit home waiting for a handout. Some of them do work."

The Mover nodded. "They do. But working and contributing aren't the same thing."

"How do you mean?"

"There's a whole subclass of Takers who actually show up," the Mover said. "They punch the clock, they stay busy, they sweat… but the job itself doesn't require anything beyond showing up. No specialization. No training. No skill that moves the world forward."

The Carrier frowned. "So they're not lazy. They're just… stuck?"

"Not stuck," the Mover replied. "Satisfied. They bring energy but not value. They bring effort but not growth. And then—here's the important part—they demand the same wages, benefits, and protections as Carriers, even though they never became one."

The Carrier leaned forward. "So they think effort equals worth."

"Exactly," the Mover said. "Effort feels noble. It feels righteous. So they believe the marketplace owes them something more because they tried hard. But the marketplace doesn't pay for effort. It pays for value."

The Carrier let out a slow breath. "And that's why they vote like Takers."

"Right again. They work like Carriers, but think like Takers. They want the rewards of skilled labor without ever learning a skill. And because there are so many of them, the system bends to their demands—usually at the expense of the actual people holding everything together."

The Carrier shook his head. "So they're workers… but still Takers."

The Mover smiled. "You're starting to see the map."

2. Carriers

"These," I said, "are the backbone of New Cheese City.
 They're the ones who actually pay for everything."

He frowned. "Everything?"

"Everything."
 "Their taxes fund the programs. Their labor supports the systems. Their compliance keeps the Rats in office. Their paychecks get drained from every angle."

He exhaled. "And they get… what?"

"Barely enough cheese to keep them walking."

Next, I tilted my head toward the frosted-glass lounge upstairs.

3. Keepers

"These are the people who own things.
 Companies.
 Assets.
 Properties.
 Systems."

"They don't *earn* cheese," I said. "They position themselves so cheese flows to them."

He nodded slowly. "So they're rich?"

"Some. But not all rich people are Keepers. Only the ones who understand how to escape the maze."

Then he asked, "And the Rats?"

I grinned.

4. Rats

"Rats don't make cheese.
 They don't own cheese.
 They don't carry cheese."

"So what do they do?"

"They negotiate cheese they never produced. They promise cheese they can't deliver. They take cheese from Carriers to give to Takers, all so Takers will keep voting for them."

He shook his head. "Sounds about right."

"And they get kickbacks from the cheese factories they regulate," I added. "To keep prices high, labor divided, and the Workers fighting among themselves."

He sat back. "Shoot."

"And that leaves one group," I said quietly.

He leaned in.

5. Movers

"Movers don't wait for cheese.
 They go find opportunity, build their own ladders, and climb right out of the maze."

"They don't fight the Rats.
 They don't envy the Keepers.
 They don't resent the Carriers.
 They don't copy the Takers."

"They build."

He stared at me for a long moment.

"So which group am I in?"

I smiled.

"That's the question most people never ask."

36

CHAPTER 4

Why the Poor Stay Poor

He shifted in his seat. "Can I ask you something? Why don't Takers just move up? Why don't they become Carriers or Movers?"

I nodded.
 "That's the question everyone asks—especially Carriers."

We watched as the little boy finally stopped crying, his mother exhausted, embarrassed, apologizing to everyone around her.

"It starts here," I said. "In childhood."

He raised an eyebrow. "Because he's spoiled?"

"No," I said. "Because he's being taught dependency."

I lowered my voice.

"Takers aren't born. They're trained.
 Just like Carriers are trained to endure.
 Just like Keepers are trained to build.
 Just like Rats are trained to manipulate."

I pointed subtly at the mother.

"She's teaching him the system she grew up in. If she lives in a world where every crisis is solved by somebody else's cheese, then that's the world he inherits."

He nodded slowly. "So it's generational."

"Exactly. And structural."

I leaned in.

"Imagine growing up in a neighborhood where almost no one works regularly. Where the cheese arrives through programs, subsidies, credits, vouchers, cards, assistance. Where survival is based on waiting."

"Waiting becomes normal.
 Wanting becomes entitlement.
 Earning becomes foreign."

He swallowed.

"And after a few generations," I continued,
"nobody respects the stores anymore. Nobody
respects the workers. Kids don't respect owners.
They don't understand why law enforcement is
always on them. They think police are hunting
them… when really, the system trained them into
the behavior that police respond to."

He sat still.

"And then," I added, "the Rats show up and tell
them:
 'It's not your fault.
 They owe you more cheese.'"

I paused.

"And the cycle resets.
 The poor stay poor.
 Not because they're incapable—
 but because the maze was built around them."

He nodded. "So how do they get out?"

I smiled sadly.

"The same way I bought my three-wheeler:
 they have to want something badly enough to earn it.
 But the system—New Cheese City—makes wanting unnecessary."

He exhaled.
"They never learn to move. Instead of change, they choose the riot—because that's what this generation calls a solution." "Exactly," I said.
 "And that's why the maze stays full."

"See, the Rats know something
Carriers don't:

You cannot tax wealth.

You can only tax income."

CHAPTER 5

Why the Rich Don't Pay Taxes

He rubbed his eyes. "Alright… tell me something. You keep saying Keepers don't pay taxes. How is that possible? Everybody pays taxes."

I grinned.
 "That's what the Rats want you to believe."

He leaned closer.

"Let me show you how New Cheese City really works."

I pointed toward the lounge upstairs.

"You see the people in that room?"

"Yeah."

"They pay less tax than the woman on her laptop down here."

He blinked. "But they're rich."

"Exactly," I said. "Because they're rich."

I could see him trying to process it.

"They don't get paid like you do," I explained. "Carriers earn **wages**, and wages get taxed into the ground. The rich earn **everything except wages** — distributions, equity, dividends, loans against assets. And those are taxed at little to zero."

He frowned. "Wait… so they really don't pay taxes?"

"They pay taxes," I said, "just not the *kind* you're thinking of."

He raised an eyebrow.

"Watch this," I said. "This will blow your mind."

I pointed to the woman on her laptop — the Carrier.

"She pays income tax, payroll tax, FICA, Social Security, Medicare, state tax if applicable, property tax, sales tax, gas tax… It never ends."

He nodded.

"Now look at the Keepers upstairs," I said. "They own companies. And companies pay payroll tax and workers' comp for every single Carrier they employ."

"So they do contribute," he said.

"Absolutely," I replied. "Corporations pay **massive** taxes.
But here's the trick:
the corporation pays them — not the Keeper personally."

I let that sit for a moment.

"The business takes the hit," I said. "Not the owner. The owner pays themselves in ways that skip personal income tax entirely."

He blinked. "Like what?"

"Like depreciation.
 Cost segregation.
 Equity payouts.
 Borrowing against assets.
 Real estate write-offs.
 Corporate vehicles.
 Corporate cards.
 Fringe benefits.
 Loss carry-forwards.
 Reinvestments."

He stared at me.

"They don't dodge taxes illegally. They dodge them *strategically*."

I continued:

"A Keeper structures their life so almost nothing qualifies as taxable income.
 And a Carrier structures their life so everything does."

He scratched his head.
 "So all those corporate taxes… don't come from the owner?"

"Nope," I said. "They come from the business."

"And the owner still gets to live like royalty."

He sat back in his seat.

"So the rich don't pay taxes… because they don't earn money the way we do."

I smiled.

"Now you're getting it."

CHAPTER 6

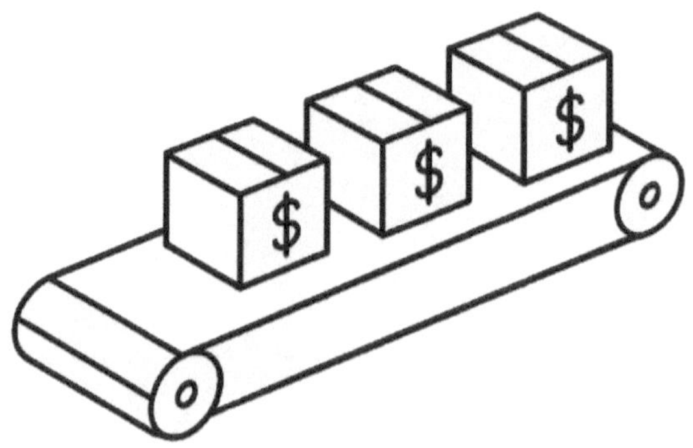

Why the Middle Class Pays for Everything

He let out a long breath.

"Okay. So the poor depend on cheese. The rich avoid taxes. The Rats manipulate everything. But why does it always feel like the middle class… gets crushed?"

I nodded.

"Because they do."

We watched as the woman in scrubs finally boarded her call, apologizing to her boss for the

delay.
 Then we looked at a guy in a reflective vest checking his bank account balance.
 Then the schoolteacher eating a $17 airport sandwich.

"These," I said softly, "are the ones paying for all of New Cheese City."

He stayed quiet.

"You know why Carriers are the most stressed?" I asked.
 "Because they make just enough to have everything taken from them… but not enough to qualify for any help."

"They pay full taxes while Keepers pay almost none.
 They fund programs Takers rely on, but they're told they make 'too much' to get assistance themselves.
 They're punished for working."

He swallowed. "So they're trapped."

"Yes," I said. "Trapped and tired."

I leaned forward.

"And the Rats *love* them this way."

He frowned. "Why would Rats want the middle class exhausted?"

"Because tired people don't fight.
 Because stressed people accept crumbs.
 Because overworked people don't read bills or track votes.
 Because overwhelmed parents don't show up to meetings.
 Because Carriers always vote for whoever promises relief — even if that relief never comes."

He nodded slowly.

"And while they're busy surviving," I continued, "Rats slide cheese to Takers to buy votes… and slide favors to Keepers to keep the money flowing."

He sank back into his seat.

"So Carriers pay for everything," he whispered.

"Yes," I said. "They are the only group that follows the rules.
 The only group that pays full price for cheese.

The only group that keeps New Cheese City running.”

“And the only group that never gets thanked for it.”

CHAPTER 7

The Great Cheese Factory Kickback Loop

He rubbed his temples.

"I still don't see how all of this keeps going. How does nobody stop it?"

I laughed softly.

"Because every group is benefiting from it… except the Carriers."

He frowned. "How?"

"Let me introduce you to the Great Cheese Factory
Kickback Loop."

Across the terminal, we saw a union worker
arguing with a non-union worker about overtime
rules at the airport café.

Perfect timing.

"Here's how it works," I said. "The Rats go to the
union workers and say:
 'Vote for us and we'll make every job a union
job.'
 This gets them kickbacks, endorsements, and
campaign power."

He nodded.

"Then the Rats walk across the street to the non-
union crowd and say the opposite:
 'Vote for us and we'll break the unions.'
 Because non-union businesses don't want to deal
with union rules."

He blinked. "So they promise both things?"

"Exactly," I said. "Whatever gets the vote."

He shook his head. "And people fall for it?"

"Every time."

"And the cheese factories?" he asked.

"Ah," I smirked. "The factories are the real winners."

"How?"

"Because they give kickbacks to the Rats to keep the price of cheese high."

I continued:

"Union workers want higher wages.
 Non-union workers want lower competition.
 Factories want bigger profits.
 Rats want both sides fighting."

He stared at me.

"That way," I said, "nobody notices who's actually getting richer."

"The Keepers," he whispered.

"Exactly. The entire fight between union and non-union is a distraction. The only group who suffers… is the Carriers. They pay higher prices, higher taxes, and higher costs."

"And the Rats cash in."

He slumped back.

"You said this airport is New Cheese City on steroids," he murmured.

"It is," I said. "And once you see it… you can't unsee it."

"Unions fight for workers.
Non-unions fight for businesses.
Rats fight for themselves,
Carriers pay the bill..."

CHAPTER 8

The Union vs. Non-Union Scam

He took a breath. "You said the union argument is a distraction. But isn't union vs. non-union a real fight? People take sides seriously."

I nodded.

"They do. And that's why Rats love it."

Across the terminal, the argument between the café
workers escalated.
 One shouted, "We deserve protection!"
 The other yelled, "We deserve freedom!"

Both passionate.
 Both convinced they were right.
 Both blind to the fact they were being used.

"Here's the truth," I said quietly.
 "In New Cheese City, neither side wins.
 Only the Rats do."

He leaned forward. "Explain."

"Unions promise higher wages, better benefits, job
security, seniority rules. Non-union shops promise
flexibility, lower costs, fewer rules, easier hiring."

"So who's right?" he asked.

"Neither," I said. "Because they're fighting the
wrong enemy."

He narrowed his eyes.
 "Who's the enemy?"

"The Rats who keep both sides angry so no one
notices the factories raising cheese prices every
year."

I continued:

"When unions get stronger, factories raise prices to 'cover increased labor costs.'
 When unions get weaker, factories still raise prices because they can."

He blinked. "So either way…"

"Carriers get crushed because they are stuck in the middle paying for everything," I said.
 "Takers don't notice because it's all free to them.
 Keepers stay untouched because either way it's higher profits for them.
 Rats will get donations from all sides."

He sat back.

"Let me put it simpler," I said.

**"Unions fight for workers.
 Non-unions fight for businesses.
 Rats fight for themselves."**

He rubbed his face.
 "And Carriers?"

"They pay the bill," I said.
 "As always."

"Free cheese destroys hunger.
Free cheese destroys ambition.
Free cheese destroys dignity."

CHAPTER 9

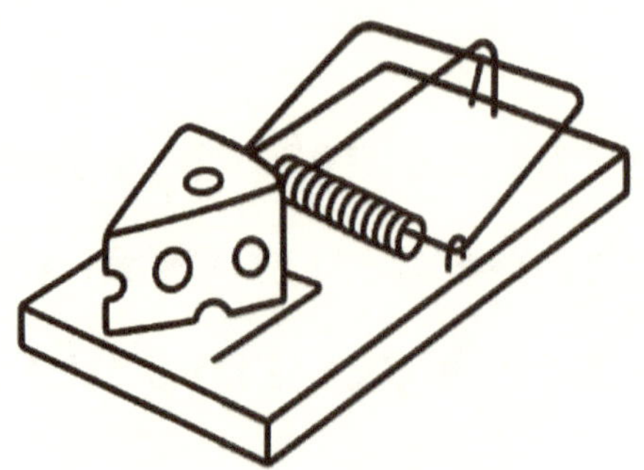

FREE CHEESE
TRAP

A family walked by — laughing, taking selfies, carrying multiple airport shopping bags.
 Another group stood in line arguing because their government travel voucher didn't cover their upgrade.

He watched the scene unfold.
 "Those people… are they Takers?"

I nodded.

"That group is. Not all poor people are Takers —
but all Takers are poor."

He frowned. "Explain."

"Takers aren't defined by income.
They're defined by mindset."

He watched them carefully now.

"They've learned the system," I continued. "They
know which forms to fill out. Which programs to
join. Which phrases to use. Which 'needs' to
emphasize. They know how to get cheese for free
— food, housing, credits, subsidies, aid."

He sighed. "And the Rats promise more every
cycle."

"Exactly. Free cheese buys votes."

Then I looked at him directly.

"But here's the trap."

He waited.

"The longer you live on free cheese,
  the more expensive the cheese becomes —
  for everyone else."

He didn't blink.

"And the more free cheese you give a city," I said,
  "the less anyone wants to work."

I pointed at the mother who had finally calmed her
child.

"You think that boy is going to grow up wanting to
earn? Or wait?"

He swallowed.

"That's the trap.
 Free cheese destroys hunger.
 Free cheese destroys ambition.
 Free cheese destroys dignity."

I leaned in slightly.

"And once you depend on the Rats for cheese…
 you will vote for them forever."

"That's why the poor stay poor," he whispered.

"No," I corrected softly.
 "That's why the poor stay *trapped*.
 Poor is a condition.
 Trapped is a system."

CHAPTER 10

The Tax-the-Rich Lie

He took a long pause, then looked me dead in the eye.

"If Keepers don't pay taxes…
and Takers don't pay taxes…
and Rats live off everyone else…
why do people fall for the 'tax the rich' line every election?"

I grinned. He was finally asking the right
questions.

"Because it feels good emotionally," I said.
 "And because it's mathematically impossible."

He waited.

"And Keepers don't earn income," he finished for me.

I nodded proudly. He was catching on fast.

"So every election," I said, "Rats stand up and say, 'We're going to tax the rich!'"

Crowds cheer.
 Signs wave.
 Carriers clap.
 Takers celebrate.

"And meanwhile," I continued, "Keepers are sitting in their lounges sipping sparkling water because they know the Rats are full of crap."

He laughed.
 "So it's all fake?"

"It's worse than fake," I corrected.

"It's a **lie** told to Carriers to make them believe someone else will finally pay for the cheese."

He looked around again — seeing the airport differently now.

"So what happens instead?"

"Carriers get taxed more.
 Sales taxes rise.
 Property taxes spike.
 Fees go up.
 Services shrink.
 Everything costs more."

"And rich people?"

"They move their money.
 Restructure their corporations.
 Shift assets.
 Change residency.
 Or leave New Cheese City entirely."

He stared down at the carpet.

"So the 'tax the rich' plan…"

"Doesn't tax the rich," I finished.

"It taxes the Carriers who believed it."

He exhaled slowly.

"And that," I said, "is why New Cheese City never changes:
 the Carriers are tricked into voting for policies
that break them."

He shook his head.

"So the Rats make promises they can't deliver, and the Carriers pay for it."

"That," I said, "is the entire model."

CHAPTER 11

The Fable:

I leaned back, watching the gate crowd swell as more flights were delayed.

"You've heard pieces," I said. "But now you need the whole story.
 Let me take you inside New Cheese City."

He nodded slowly.

"Alright," I said.
 "Here's how the city worked."

THE TAKERS

"New Cheese City had entire neighborhoods built
on free cheese.
 Generations deep."

People lived in the same apartments their parents
had lived in.

Programs paid the rent.
 Cards covered the food.
 Stipends covered the school supplies.
 Vouchers covered the gas.
 Subsidies covered the bills.

The only skill most residents learned…
 was how to navigate the forms that kept the
cheese flowing.

No one taught them how to earn.
 No one taught them entrepreneurship.
 No one taught them escape.

Kids grew up watching their parents wait in lines.
 Fight store owners.
 Blame the police.
 Blame the neighbors.
 Blame anyone but themselves.

And they inherited that mindset.

Takers weren't lazy.
 They were trained.
 The maze built walls around them before they
could even walk.

THE CARRIERS

"All the while," I continued,
 "Carriers kept the city alive."

They were the nurses, the airport workers, the
teachers, the construction crews, the servers, the
truck drivers, the clerks.

They worked two jobs to afford one life.

They paid every tax.
 They followed every rule.
 They showed up early.
 They stayed late.
 They apologized for things that weren't their fault.

And every year, they were told:

> "If you want better cheese, work
> harder."

So they did.
 And the taxes went up.
 And the prices went up.
 And the assistance they didn't qualify for
expanded for everyone else.

They carried the city — literally.

But no matter how hard they worked, they were never allowed in the room where cheese decisions were made.

THE KEEPERS

"Up in the towers," I said, "lived the Keepers."

They didn't run stores.
 They didn't clock in.
 They didn't pick up overtime.
 They didn't deal with customers.

They owned the land the stores sat on.
 They owned the buildings Carriers worked in.
 They owned the companies Rats negotiated with.

They didn't walk through the maze.

They owned the walls.

And because of the structure they created, they legally paid almost no personal taxes.

The corporations they owned paid taxes.
 The workers they hired paid taxes.
 The customers who bought their products paid taxes.

But the Keepers?

They floated.

Above the noise.
 Above the fights.
 Above the struggle.

They operated through companies based in the
next state — avoiding local taxes entirely.
 They lived in quiet suburbs outside New Cheese
City while profiting from everything inside it.

THE RATS

"And then," I said,
 "There were the Rats."

Rats ran the place.

They took kickbacks from the Keepers, the Unions
and the Non-Unions.
 They promised cheese to the Takers.
 They scolded the Carriers for not carrying enough.
 They told the Non-Union Workers they'd break
unions.

They told the Union Workers they'd strengthen unions.

They promised to tax the rich.
 They never did, because they couldn't.

They promised free cheese to the poor.
 They delivered just enough to win the next vote.

They promised relief to the middle class.
 They delivered nothing but the taxes to pay for free cheese.

And every election, they told every group what they wanted to hear.

To the Takers:
 "You deserve more."

To the Carriers:
 "You're not paying enough."

To the Keepers:
 "We'll keep the system stable."

And with every promise, every lie, every manufactured fight…

the Rats grew fatter.

Off cheese they never made.

THE MOVERS

"Finally," I continued,
 "There were the Movers."

They lived in New Cheese City…
 but the city did not live inside them.

They learned skills the system couldn't tax.
 They found opportunities the Rats couldn't
manipulate.
 They built side businesses, online ventures,
consulting gigs, trades, investments.

They created value.

Then they built ladders.
 Climbed walls.
 And walked right out of the maze.

They weren't rich yet — not like the Keepers —
 but they were free in a way almost no one else
was.

And as they rose, they reached back and helped
people who were ready to move too.

Not Takers.
 Not the entitled.
 Not the complainers.

But people hungry for something more.

Movers didn't fight the system.

They outgrew it.

THE COLLAPSE OF NEW CHEESE CITY

"And then," I said,
 "New Cheese City began to crack."

Cheese prices soared because the factories kept
raising them.
 Carriers struggled because taxes kept rising.
 Keepers moved money out of the city.
 Takers demanded more than the city could give.

And Rats kept promising everything…
 while delivering nothing.

Eventually, something broke.

The Carriers began to leave.

The only group who truly paid for the cheese
 packed up, moved out, or became Movers.

And without the Carriers…

New Cheese City collapsed.

Not suddenly.
 Not explosively.

But quietly.
 Inevitably.
 Predictably.

Because once the middle class stops carrying,
 the whole maze falls.

He stared at me for a long time.

"That's… brutal."

"No," I said. "That's reality."

He swallowed.

"And that," I added,
 "is New Cheese City."

CHAPTER 12

Back to the Terminal:
Everything Makes Sense Now

He sat still for nearly a full minute.

Then he said, almost in a whisper:

"…It's real, isn't it?"

I nodded.
"You've lived in New Cheese City your whole life."

He looked around.

At the scrubs-wearing Carrier apologizing into her phone.

At the exhausted father digging for snacks for his kids.

At the Taker family laughing with bags full of airport souvenirs they didn't pay for.

At the lounge above us full of people who didn't even hear the gate change.

At the politician taking selfies with strangers.

At the workers sweeping, checking, organizing, cleaning.

He wiped his palms against his jeans.

"Holy crap," he said. "It really is New Cheese City."

I nodded.

He leaned back, absorbing everything.

"The maze," he whispered.

"Yep."

"The cheese signs."

"Yep."

"The Rats. The Keepers. The Carriers. The Takers…"

"And the Movers," I added.

He glanced at me.

"Which one are you?"

I smiled slowly.

"A Mover.
 Used to be a Carrier.
 Could have become a Taker.
 Was never meant to be a Keeper."

He laughed nervously.
 "So… how did you move?"

"One decision at a time," I said.
 "All rooted in the same lesson my mom gave me
with that three-wheeler."

He waited.

"If you want something badly enough," I said
softly,
 "you will figure out a way to earn it."

He nodded slowly.

"And once you figure that out," I said,
 "you stop looking for free cheese.

You stop blaming the Rats.
You stop fighting the Keepers.
You stop comparing yourself to Carriers.
You stop resenting Takers."

"You start moving."

He exhaled.

"Now you see the city," I said.
"Now you understand the maze."

"And once you see it…
you can't unsee it."

CHAPTER 13

The Path Out of the Maze

"So how do I do it?" he asked.
 "How do I get out of the maze?"

I smiled.
 "This is where most people get it wrong."

He leaned in.

"They think escaping the maze requires rebellion.
 Revolution.
 Fighting the system.
 Burning it down.
 Electing new Rats.
 Taxing Keepers.
 Punishing Takers."

He nodded. "That's what everybody argues about."

"And that," I said, "is why nobody escapes."

I paused to let it sink in.

"You don't escape the maze by changing the maze.
 You escape by changing yourself."

He stared at me.

"The maze is designed to react to frustration.
 It absorbs anger.
 It feeds off blame.
 It grows stronger when people fight inside it."

"So what do I do?" he asked again.

"You take the Mover path."

"What's that?"

"The only path the Rats can't regulate.
 The only path the Keepers can't control.
 The only path Takers won't take.
 The only path Carriers were never taught."

He waited.

"You learn a skill.
 A real skill.
 Not a degree.

Not a certification.
A skill that creates value."

"Then you use that skill to build something small
—
a service, a product, a side income. Many of the companies you recognize today were started with little to no money. It's not about money, it's about mindset."

"You reinvest.
You grow.
You build leverage."

"And once you build leverage…"

"You climb."

He swallowed.

"And once you climb…"

"You move."

He sat back slowly.

"So escaping New Cheese City isn't about politics?"

"No," I said. "It's about power."

"If you want something badly
enough,
you will find a way to earn it."

CHAPTER 14

The Three-Wheeler Lesson

He stared at me, absorbing everything.

"Was that how you did it?" he asked.
"With the skill thing? The ladder thing?"

I chuckled.
"No. It started way earlier than that. It started the day I wanted a three-wheeler."

He tilted his head.
"You mentioned that earlier."

"Yeah," I said. "Let me tell you the full story."

I leaned back in my chair.

"I was five. I saw a three-wheeled bike in a store window. Bright yellow. Plastic wheels. Dumb little handlebar streamers. The most beautiful thing I'd ever seen."

He smiled.

"I told my mom I wanted it. Expected her to say yes. Expected her to do what every kid-trained Taker gets taught."

He nodded. "Buy it."

"Yep."

"But she didn't even blink. She just said,
 'If you really want that bike, figure out a way to buy it.'"

He laughed.
 "Bet that shocked you."

"I thought it was insane," I said. "I had thirty-five cents a month in allowance. I had nothing saved. Back then, nobody gave money for birthdays."

"So what did you do?"

"What she taught me to do," I said. "Earn it."

I worked in my parents' bakery on weekends
sweeping floors, stacking trays, cleaning tables. I
helped neighbors rake leaves or pull weeds. I
saved every penny."

"How long did it take?"

"Months. But one day, I walked back into that
store with every dollar in my hand — twenty-five
bucks — and I bought the bike myself."

I paused.

"And that day changed everything.
 Not because of the bike — that thing didn't last, it
had plastic wheels for crying out loud."

He laughed.

"But because I learned the most important lesson
New Cheese City doesn't want you to know."

I turned toward him.

**"If you want something badly enough,
 you will find a way to earn it."**

He nodded slowly.

"That one lesson," I said, "can turn a Taker into a Carrier…
 and a Carrier into a Mover."

I tapped the armrest between us.

"And it's why New Cheese City is collapsing.
 Too many people were never told what my mom told me."

CHAPTER 15

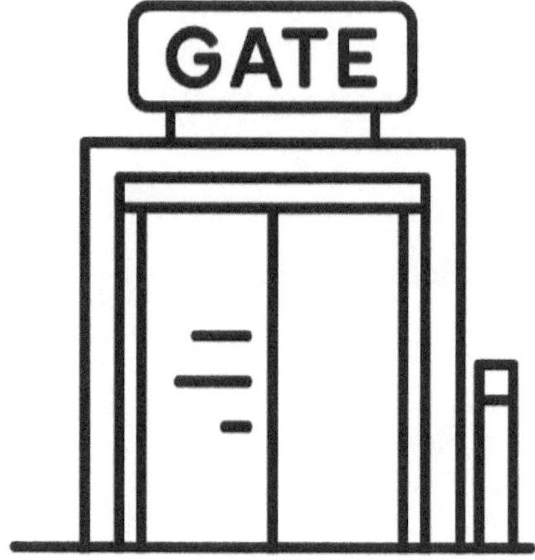

The Final Boarding Call:
What Happens If We Don't Change?

A new announcement echoed overhead.

"Attention passengers, final boarding for Flight 627…"

The guy beside me checked his phone.
 "We've been talking for hours. It felt like ten minutes."

I nodded.
 "That's what happens when you finally see the system from above."

He leaned back and stared at the ceiling.

"So what happens," he asked quietly,
 "if nobody becomes a Mover?
 If everyone just stays in the maze?"

I didn't sugarcoat it.

"New Cheese City collapses."

He swallowed.
 "How?"

"Piece by piece," I said.

"When Keepers feel the system turning unstable — they move their money out."

"When Takers demand more than the system can give — programs buckle."

"When Rats get desperate — they make reckless promises."

"When factories raise cheese prices — inflation crushes the Carriers."

"When Carriers get tired enough — they either leave or stop carrying."

"And once the Carriers stop carrying…"

I paused.

"…the entire maze falls apart."

He stared at me.

"Is that where we are now?"

I nodded slowly.

"We're at final boarding call."

He looked around the terminal like he was seeing ghosts.

"The free cheese is running out.
 The Carriers are drowning.
 The Keepers are withdrawing.
 The Rats are panicking."

"And unless more people become Movers…"

I let the silence finish the sentence for me.

He exhaled.

"So it's not about saving New Cheese City."

"No," I said. "It's about saving yourself."

"And if enough people save themselves…"

"New Cheese City saves itself by accident," I finished.

Leaving New Cheese City

The airport finally quieted as the last delayed flights took off into the night sky.

The Carrier sat beside me — no longer confused, no longer angry, just awake.

We had watched the Takers, the Carriers, the Keepers, the Rats, and even the Movers walk past us in real time.

Now they understood the maze.
 Now they understood the cheese.
 Now they understood their role.

The Carrier finally asked the question everyone asks eventually:

"…Is it really possible to leave?"

I stood and picked up my bag.

"Yes," I said.
 "But you don't leave by fighting.
 You leave by outgrowing."

He waited.

"You stop waiting for cheese.
 You stop begging for relief.
 You stop blaming the system.
 You stop voting for promises."

"You learn a skill.
 You build something.
 You keep what you earn.
 You move."

Another announcement sounded:

"Final boarding…"

I turned back to him.

"New Cheese City only controls the people who wait for someone else to decide their worth."

"Movers stop waiting."

I walked toward my gate — not because I was escaping the city…

…but because I had outgrown it years ago.

The Escape Blueprint

If the entire book had to be summed up in one page, this is it:

1. Stop Waiting.

Free cheese is a trap.
 Dependence is control.

2. Stop Blaming.

Blame feeds Rats.
 Movers focus on building.

3. Stop Asking for What You Didn't Earn.

The more you depend on the maze, the deeper it pulls you in.

4. Start Learning How the System Works.

Money flows to value — not effort.
 Taxes punish wages — not wealth.

5. Start Moving.

Movement is mental before it's financial.

6. Start Building a Skill.

A skill is untaxable leverage.

7. Start Creating Your Own Cheese.

Not wages.
 Not programs.
 Not promises.
 Value.

8. Start Helping Others Who Want to Climb.

Movers create more Movers.

9. Start Living Outside the Maze.

Your life is bigger than New Cheese City.

10. Start Today.

Not tomorrow.
 Not after payday.
 Not after the next election.

Today.

ABOUT THE AUTHOR

Eric F. Gilbert is an entrepreneur, author, marketer, and mentor who has spent decades helping people break out of systems designed to keep them trapped. Through books, training, business ownership, and media, he has taught thousands how to escape dependency, build value, and rise beyond the maze.

From designing businesses to exposing how modern economics really works, Eric's mission is simple:

Help people stop waiting for cheese — and start making their own.

He lives in Florida with his wife, where they run multiple companies, create content, and continue helping others build lives beyond New Cheese City.